ACCESS THE ACTION!

Scan the QR code to
hear this story for
FREE!

Published in the UK by Sweet Cherry Publishing Limited, 2025
Unit 4u18, The Book Brothers Business Park,
Tolwell Road, Leicester LE4 1BR, United Kingdom

Unit 31, The Pottery, Bakers Point,
Pottery Road, Dún Laoghaire,
Dublin A96 EV18, Ireland

SWEET CHERRY and associated logos are trademarks and/or
registered trademarks of Sweet Cherry Publishing Limited.

2 4 6 8 10 9 7 5 3 1

ISBN: 978-1-80263-469-3

Football Rising Stars: Lee Kang-in

© Sweet Cherry Publishing Limited, 2025

Text by Harry Meredith
Illustrations by Sophie Jones

All rights reserved. No part of this publication may be reproduced
or utilised in any form or by any means, electronic or mechanical,
including photocopying, recording, or using any information storage
and retrieval system, without prior permission in writing from the
publisher. No part of this publication may be used or reproduced
in any manner for the purpose of training artificial intelligence
technologies or systems.

The right of Harry Meredith to be identified as the author of
this work has been asserted by them in accordance with
the Copyright, Designs and Patents Act 1988.

This book is not authorised, licensed or approved by Lee Kang-in.
Any faults are the publisher's, who will be happy to rectify
for future printings.

www.sweetcherrypublishing.com

Printed and bound in India

LEE KANG-IN

THE UNOFFICIAL STORY

Written by
HARRY MEREDITH

Sweet Cherry

CONTENTS

1. Korea Republic — 7
2. Fly Shoot Dori — 18
3. Boy Wonder — 25
4. Spanish Dream — 32
5. Valencia CF Academy — 38
6. Valencia Mestalla — 46
7. Los Ches — 55
8. The Golden Ball — 65
9. The Hurdle — 77
10. RCD Mallorca — 84
11. World Cup 2022 — 91
12. Paris Saint-Germain — 108
13. Asian Games — 117
14. Hope and Belief — 124

1
KOREA REPUBLIC

On the 16th of November 2023, over 64,000 excited fans took their seats in the Seoul World Cup Stadium. They had purchased tickets to watch an electrifying World Cup qualifier between South Korea (known as Korea Republic) and Singapore.

★ FOOTBALL RISING STARS ★

The two countries were opening their campaigns for the 2026 World Cup, ready to stake their claim as one of the Asian Football Confederation representatives. While a victory in this match would not book their place in the famous competition, one team could push themselves closer. Both sides were willing to fight with everything they had to take their country to the 2026 World Cup.

Korea Republic were the home team, playing in their nation's capital, which gave them an advantage. Most fans in attendance were wearing the country's colours and cheering the team on. They were the clear favourites for the match, but nothing in football is ever certain.

In order to triumph, Korea Republic would need to rely on their talented roster. Son Heung-min, the country's superstar forward, was captaining the side. There were also other experienced heads such as Lee Jae-sung, Kim Young-gwon and Kim Seung-gyu. However, the match would not exclusively be decided by the team's elders.

★ FOOTBALL RISING STARS ★

Lee Kang-in, the youngest player on the roster, was one of the most exciting prospects to emerge from the country in quite some time. Playing his club football with Paris Saint-Germain, he was a young star at the top of European football. Could he help his country succeed?

Korea Republic were playing in their traditional red, against Singapore who were playing in blue. The home team applied the pressure, trying their hardest to find a way through, but a strong and stubborn Singaporean defence refused to be broken.

⋆★ LEE KANG-IN ★⋆

Kang-in and his teammates led wave after wave of attacks in the first half, with their efforts being saved, blocked or just missing the target. In fact, one effort thwacked against the crossbar! The Singapore players were giving everything to keep the score level.

As the final minutes of the first half were coming to an end, Korea Republic found themselves with one huge chance.

Son passed the ball to Kang-in, who looked up and saw a line of defenders and a couple of attacking red shirts.

 Many players would think there was no way forward, but Kang-in had other ideas. He played a precise lofted through ball over the defence, causing the fans to rise from their seats in anticipation. Cho Gue-sung followed the ball's flight and calmly slotted it into the back of the net. Korea Republic had the lead!

The players celebrated, and Cho pointed at Kang-in and praised him for his accurate assist.

The first half came to a close, and Kang-in and his teammates headed

★ LEE KANG-IN ★

into the changing room with a promising advantage.

Having finally made the breakthrough, Korea Republic came out into the second half more determined than ever.

Singapore would need to carry out further attacks if they wanted to get back into the match, which could lead to there being more space for the Korea Republic attackers to play with. This would set up room for the team's creatives to do what they did best: create goals and assists with the magic of their feet, or move between the lines and make devastating passes.

With this freedom, Korea Republic put on a show for the thousands in attendance. Hwang Hee-chan scored the team's second goal in the 49th minute with a header. Son added a third goal to the scoresheet in the 63rd minute – a long-range strike with his left foot that curled into the top corner – and Hwang Ui-jo scored the team's fourth from the penalty spot.

Kang-in had worked tirelessly through the match. He had earned an assist and played a huge role in the team's success, yet there were still a handful of minutes to play. The scoring in this match was not quite finished.

A cross from the left-hand side of the pitch was headed away by a Singaporean defender, but their attempted clearance fell to the feet of Kang-in. He looked up and fired a rocket of a shot towards the goal. The goalkeeper could do nothing as the ball flew past him and into the net. Kang-in had scored, and Korea Republic were 5-0 up!

Exhausted from his hard work, Kang-in didn't run or cheer when he scored. Instead, he calmly high-fived his teammates as they congratulated him on his goal.

A few minutes later, the referee brought the match to an end. Korea Republic took all three points. The entertaining and high-scoring match was one their fans would remember for a long time!

Kang-in and his team had earned an impressive victory to start their journey to the 2026 World Cup, to fight for their spot in the tournament.

★ LEE KANG-IN ★

With some of their talented roster coming towards the ends of their careers, Korea Republic needed fresh players who could lead them to new heights. Kang-in had shown just how capable he was of doing that.

At the age of twenty-two, Kang-in had a lot of football still to play. If he could score, assist and put in performances like that, then the future of the team was in good hands. Korea Republic had a star for now and the future.

2
FLY SHOOT DORI

Lee Kang-in was born on the 19th of February 2001 in the city of Incheon in South Korea.

His father, Lee Woon-seong, was a taekwondo instructor and a huge football fan. He passed down this joy and admiration for the sport to his son, often showing Kang-in videos of his favourite footballers – one of them being the Argentinian legend Diego Maradona.

Small in stature but enormous in legacy, Maradona was a tricky forward who could run rings around defences and scored goals for fun. Kang-in was inspired by Maradona and wanted to play as an attacker himself, scoring and creating goals for his team.

Kang-in practised playing football with his father, using any spare time he could find to work on his skills. As a result of this, Kang-in's life changed dramatically when he was six years old.

Having picked up some early footballing promise, the young boy applied for a South Korean reality show called *Fly Shoot Dori*. The show was a feature on one of the country's main broadcasters, KBS, and was beamed onto millions of TV screens across the country every year. It followed a group of young boys with varying football

abilities as they trained and played together, becoming a team under the guidance of established coaches and actors.

One of those coaches was a former South Korean football icon, Yoo Sang-chul. Yoo was famous for playing his part in the country's best ever performance at the 2002 World Cup (when South Korea hosted), helping the team make it all the way to the semi-final. He even earned himself a spot in the Team of the Tournament after the competition ended.

Out of the hundreds of children

who applied to be on season three of *Fly Shoot Dori*, Kang-in was chosen! He was very grateful for the opportunity to learn from some of the country's best, developing his abilities in front of the cameras and in view of an entire nation willing him to succeed.

Kang-in excelled in the show, even becoming a mini-celebrity in his country. Everyone watching thought he was a talented and charming young boy.

But it wasn't just his charm and kindness that won viewers over.

⭐ LEE KANG-IN ⭐

Kang-in also displayed an incredible talent and desire to play football, showing abilities that amazed all spectators and coaches alike. In many matches, Kang-in would run the show for his team.

In one match where the team were beating their opponents by a large margin, the coaches decided to make it fairer by putting Kang-in in goal. After a while, they allowed him to do what he wanted again.

Still wearing his goalkeeping

gloves, and still playing as the team's goalkeeper, six-year-old Kang-in collected the ball at the back and charged forward. He ran through the opposition team and scored an amazing goal.

Kang-in was a football superstar, showing remarkable promise at such a young age. He helped his team triumph in the show, and at the end of the season he earned a reward. It was the chance to star in an advert with another of the country's football icons: Park Ji-sung.

3
BOY WONDER

After triumphing in *Fly Shoot Dori*, Kang-in was flown over to England as a reward. Being too young to go by himself, Kang-in's mother went with him for the visit. The pair of them were excited for a new adventure, and to meet South Korean legend Park Ji-sung. Kang-in couldn't wait to star in the advert with him!

In addition to playing for the Korea Republic national team, Park was a Manchester United player. A tenacious midfielder who never shied away from working hard, he gave his all in every match. He controlled the centre of the pitch, allowing his teammates to attack with creativity and freedom. His energy and work ethic had helped Manchester United enjoy a golden era of football. Park was part of a dominant team managed by Sir

Alex Ferguson, and he won trophies galore during his stint with the club. He'd played alongside Wayne Rooney, Nemanja Vidić, Ruud van Nistelrooy, Cristiano Ronaldo and many more great Manchester United players.

Kang-in had a great time filming the advert. Not unfamiliar with cameras, he was a natural and fitted in well. He was a star in his own right next to one of the greats of South Korean football.

Eventually, it was time for Kang-in to fly back home after an exciting trip. He wanted to push on from his time at *Fly Shoot Dori* and develop his football skills away from the spotlight.

Kang-in's talents put him on the radar of many youth teams after the show ended, but he wanted to work on his skills closer to home.

He chose to play for Incheon United's youth team, a professional football club in South Korea.

Alongside other talented players in his age group, Kang-in worked on his game and played at his very best. Just as he had in the show, he displayed a level that could not be matched.

★ LEE KANG-IN ★

None of the other children could compare in ability to him.

And so, after some time, Kang-in moved to Flyings FC to see how he would do. But it was the same story! Despite playing against the top players in the area, Kang-in wasn't being challenged enough. It was amazing to win almost every match and score countless goals, but Kang-in's constant success was actually slowing his progress.

If he stayed in his home country, Kang-in knew what to expect.

After developing in an academy, he could become a legendary player for a club in the K League – the top professional football league in South Korea.

But there was always going to be something wrong with that fantasy.

Kang-in's coaches truly believed that there was limitless potential in this boy wonder. If Kang-in was going to achieve his promise, he would need to leave the comforts of his own home and head overseas to develop in an established academy programme – most likely in Europe.

Only then could he truly push his abilities and learn from the best football coaches in the world.

At the age of ten, Kang-in had a decision to make. Was he happy to stay at home and play in South Korea? Or was he going to be brave and fly thousands of miles away in the pursuit of greatness?

It was a difficult decision for a young boy to make, so he needed guidance from his family, friends and coaches. After all, his choice would shape his future in the world of football.

4
SPANISH DREAM

After careful consideration, Kang-in made up his mind. He was going to do everything he could to become the best he could be – even if that meant making sacrifices. He was going to try and make it as a professional footballer outside of South Korea.

⋆ **LEE KANG-IN** ⋆

With the help of his coaches, Kang-in was put in touch with a handful of Spanish academies.

At ten years old, Kang-in set off on an adventure thousands of miles away from home. He would need to impress in order to secure an opportunity. And while Kang-in did not speak Spanish, he wasn't worried. He was going to let his skill and ability do the talking. After all, football talent isn't limited by language – it is an art that can be understood by everyone! When a magician has a ball at their feet, it is always mesmerising to watch.

Kang-in dazzled during his trials and was offered an opportunity with Valencia CF. This was his chance to join and develop within a top academy setup for a side playing in La Liga (Spain's first division). However, his offer did come with conditions.

Being just ten years old, Kang-in couldn't simply move to Spain on his own. Instead, his entire  family would need to move with him. Not only for training, but

 for legal reasons too. A club cannot just recruit a talented international minor, as there are strict rules and regulations in youth football about the protection of the child.

Kang-in's parents needed time to consider the offer. It was an incredible opportunity for their son, but it was also a decision that would greatly impact their lives. They would need to move continents and settle in a country where they didn't speak the language or have any familiarity.

But in the end, they knew exactly what they needed to do. They wanted the best for their son and they believed this was the right thing for Kang-in. The family would be taking this massive step forward together, leaving South Korea and settling in the Spanish city of Valencia.

After Kang-in said goodbye to his teammates and coaches in South Korea, his entire family tried to squeeze as much of their old lives as they could into suitcases. It was time

⋆✦ LEE KANG-IN ✦⋆

for them all to leave their beloved home and board an aeroplane, setting off on the adventure of a lifetime.

5
VALENCIA CF ACADEMY

Upon arrival, the family settled in Puçol in Valencia. It was a home that would work for everyone. Kang-in would be able to easily travel to training sessions and matches, and there was access to shops, supermarkets, schools and jobs nearby.

⋆✸ LEE KANG-IN ✸⋆

The language barrier, while difficult, was something that Kang-in was determined to overcome quickly. After being enrolled into a local school, he wanted to understand what was happening around him and enthusiastically tried to learn the language.

So that Kang-in could easily communicate with his teammates, the academy also helped him learn Spanish. With communication being an important and effective part of

football, he needed to contribute to the team by strategising and alerting other players to danger – turning a team of eleven individuals into a collective working towards the same goal.

But while efforts were being made to improve communication, that's not to say that the language barrier didn't cause problems.

Due to a misunderstanding about his age, the club placed Kang-in in the year group above his own when he first arrived. This meant that Kang-in had to face off against players with a year's more experience than him, both from a mental and physical perspective, which added another layer of complexity and challenge to his academy football.

But Kang-in had faced bigger challenges than this, and he was not going to let anything stand in his way.

Despite these disadvantages, he quickly showed his coaches why so many people had believed in him and encouraged the boy wonder to push himself further. He was a gem with unlimited potential.

Kang-in was proving himself on the training pitches, but he didn't let football consume him. He always tried his best in school and wanted to learn as much as he could, ensuring that he put as much effort into revision and studying as he did into football matches. If he wanted to carve out a successful and fulfilling future for himself and his family, he knew he needed to work very hard and make the most of every opportunity he was given. One day, he hoped to repay his family for sacrificing so much for his dreams and ambitions.

✦★ LEE KANG-IN ★✦

Kang-in was a star for the academy, progressing through each year group and developing with his peers. As each year passed, he picked up more skills to add to his list. He was naturally quick and had always loved running past defenders, but in the academy he was able to work on a number of attributes.

Learning in a country famed for possession football, Kang-in was always encouraged to do things the Spanish way and play the extra pass. His coaches told him to prioritise possession within a game, starving opposition teams of the ball so that they couldn't get any chances to begin with.

Kang-in also learnt how to slowly and methodically help his team work their way up the pitch, creating the best opportunities for a goal. Never rushing, but always taking care of the ball.

Most importantly, he also learnt to play with flare and fun.

Kang-in took the Spanish attitude to football and combined it with his own experiences, bringing his abilities and development to another level as he progressed within the academy. Some players were let go, but Kang-in always remained a part of the year group, gradually making his way closer and closer to the professional game.

6
VALENCIA MESTALLA

In the Spanish football pyramid, clubs are allowed to have B teams. B teams are reserve squads that can compete within a professional league in the country. However, that reserve team can never be promoted to the same tier as the

★ LEE KANG-IN ★

A team – also known as the first team.

Spain are not the only country to adopt this model, but this type of league structure is divisive across the world of football. Some argue that this structure disadvantages new clubs lower down in the pyramid, making it more difficult for them to compete at a higher level, while others argue that this system provides invaluable experience for younger players. By learning in the lower leagues, in the hope of making it all the way to the top one day, young talents are more likely to reach the professional game sooner.

✦★ FOOTBALL RISING STARS ★✦

Having excelled in the academy, joining Valencia's B team was the next step for Kang-in. In late 2017, the coaches believed that it was finally his time. Kang-in was offered a contract to play for Valencia B, otherwise known as Valencia Mestalla, and represent the club in the lower Spanish divisions.

Kang-in was given his debut in a 1-1 draw against RZ Deportivo Aragòn.

He was only on the field for a handful of minutes, but Kang-in could now say he was officially a footballer. He was

★ LEE KANG-IN ★

a player with an appearance for Valencia B in a professional football league.

As a young boy in South Korea, Kang-in dreamt of becoming a professional football player. He tried and trained as much as he could to achieve his dreams and now they had come true! He hadn't imagined making his debut in the third tier of the Spanish football pyramid, but it didn't matter. It was the fact that he had made a debut at all.

Kang-in had beaten the odds and made his way into the professional game. He had not overcome every hurdle, as nothing in football is ever guaranteed, but he had achieved a lifelong dream.

Kang-in loved this feeling, and he couldn't wait to experience more of it while he developed with Valencia B.

In his debut season, the 2017/2018 campaign, Kang-in was frequently used as a substitute, earning more minutes on the pitch and gradually increasing those minutes as the season progressed. Nine minutes turned to fourteen, fourteen became fifty-eight. By the end of the season Kang-in was playing every last second, fighting for the team over the course of an entire ninety-minute match.

In the club's final home game of the season, a fixture against CE Sabadell FC, Kang-in was able to tick off another achievement on his wish list. He scored his first professional goal, and the team's first of the match, to help his side to a 2-0 victory. Valencia B ended the campaign in eleventh place –

 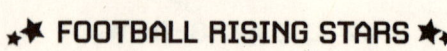

a commendable finish in a twenty-team league, but with plenty of room for improvement in the following season.

Kang-in and his teammates returned for the 2018/2019 season, hoping to develop and improve upon the previous year.

Match by match, Kang-in did exactly that, troubling opposition defences and leading his team to victory. He earned appearances in the league as well as chances to represent the team in the UEFA Youth League

LEE KANG-IN

– a developmental competition for younger players, similar to the Champions League.

No matter the game, Kang-in impressed. Not only did he impress his Valencia B coaches, but he also impressed the coaches and management of Valencia as an entire club.

Slowly but surely, rumours started to spread that he had done enough to earn an appearance for the first team, Valencia CF, in the top division – and all while he was still only a teenager!

Although Kang-in tried his best not to focus on the rumours, he still thought about what it would feel like to play at the highest level.

However, he couldn't control rumours that might not even be true. All he could control was how hard he trained, preparing for his moment in the spotlight.

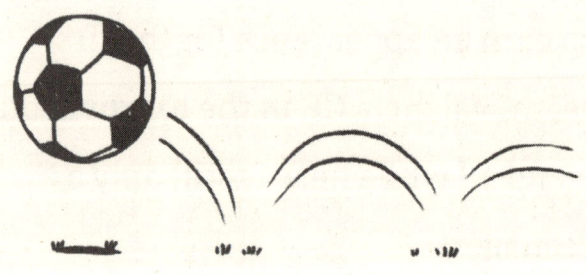

7
LOS CHES

Almost every football team has a nickname. Some earn theirs through the colours of their kits or from famous players in the past.

Valencia's nickname, Los Ches, represents the people of the city. 'Che' is an informal way of saying hello in the region, and it is not used anywhere else in the country. It's a unique expression that represents the city the team plays for – a warm and welcoming club that had become Kang-in's home.

The team had taken him in as a boy and helped him develop into a young man, learning the Valencian way as he continuously made his way through the team's ranks.

In 2018, having impressed for Valencia B, Kang-in was going to do something he had dreamt of ever since he stepped foot in the city.

★ LEE KANG-IN ★

He was going to get to play for the first team! To wear the famous orange of Valencia and represent the club's thousands of supporters was a huge honour.

Kang-in was named in the squad on the 30th of October 2018 – not in La Liga, but in a Spanish domestic cup competition called the Copa del Rey.

The exciting and valuable tournament can work wonders for a team and their fans. With league titles being hard to come by, with Real Madrid and Barcelona often dominating, the Copa del Rey is where other teams have a better chance of winning silverware. It is an opportunity to celebrate and enjoy a successful season, to go on a cup run that ignites the passion and dreams of the club's fans.

Kang-in earned his debut in the first match of the tournament, becoming one of the youngest South Korean football players to debut in Europe, and played for the majority of the game. While he did not score or assist, his tireless

✦ **LEE KANG-IN** ✦

work helped lead the side to a 1-2 victory against CD Ebro.

After having made his debut for the team, Kang-in felt incredibly proud. His friends and family celebrated him, congratulating Kang-in on making it all the way. The sacrifices and hard work were all starting to pay off. The South Korean boy wonder had turned into a professional football player. With so much ahead of him, there were no limits to what else Kang-in could achieve.

Kang-in also earned himself some La Liga and Europa League appearances in his debut season, playing in matches against Real Valladolid, Villarreal, Levante and Celtic.

He was used sparingly by the coaches, who were wary about exposing him to too much too soon, but he was allowed to train with the first team squad and gain invaluable experience from some of the club's stars. There was Dani Parejo, Carlos Soler, Gonçalo Guedes, Kevin

✦ LEE KANG-IN ✦

Gameiro and Rodrigo – a host of talented and experienced players that Kang-in could learn from.

Yet the new recruit to the squad was not the only fresh face.

Kang-in had risen through the academy in a similar time frame as Ferran Torres, a tricky winger who was seen as one of Spain's most exciting young talents. Torres had shown that it was possible for an academy prospect to thrive in a first team environment, and Kang-in really

hoped that he could achieve the same thing.

Valencia enjoyed an impressive campaign in the 2018/2019 season. The side finished in fourth place in La Liga, earning qualification for the 2019/2020 Champions League.

They also did exceptionally well in the Europa League, making it all the way to the semi-final before coming up against and losing to a stubborn Arsenal side.

But it was in the Copa del Rey, the competition Kang-in had made his

⋆★ LEE KANG-IN ★⋆

first team debut in, where the club enjoyed the most success.

After CD Ebro, the team overcame Sporting Gijón, Getafe and Real Betis, making it all the way to the final of the competition. Kang-in had played a part in the majority of the team's matches, putting himself in contention for an appearance in the final.

However, there was one slight problem with this.

The final would be taking place at the end of the season on the 25th of May 2019, but Kang-in had been called up for another exciting opportunity on the very same day.

As a result of his development, he had been called up to represent his home nation, Korea Republic, at the U20 World Cup in Poland.

8
THE GOLDEN BALL

Kang-in had always been on the radar of the Korea Republic team. Ever since his rise to fame with *Fly Shoot Dori*, he was seen as a boy wonder who could one day represent his country – a future star who could lead his nation to success and glory.

 ★ **FOOTBALL RISING STARS** ★

He had taken part in training camps and matches with the Korea Republic youth teams, and now it was his turn for an international tournament. He finally had the opportunity to represent his country and see just how far Korea Republic could go in a very exciting U20 World Cup.

Korea Republic had been placed in Group F, where the team would be competing against Portugal, South Africa and Argentina for a place in the knock-out rounds. It was a tough group, but the players had a lot of faith in one another. They believed that if they played at their best, as a collective rather than as individuals, they could get out of the group.

The country's first match was against Portugal. The team tried their hardest, but unfortunately their opening game didn't go to plan. They lost 1-0 to Portugal, conceding an early goal that they couldn't recover from.

While frustrated, Kang-in knew that the day was far from over.

That same evening, in front of a crowd of 53,698 fans at the Benito Villamarín Stadium in Seville, Valencia would be playing against Barcelona in the Copa del Rey final.

Kang-in couldn't attend because he was in Poland. But as the players rested after their opening match, desperate to put their opening defeat behind them, Kang-in and many of his teammates came together to watch the game.

If Valencia could overcome the Spanish giant, Barcelona, and win the trophy, Kang-in would receive his first ever professional winner's medal. Although he could not play in the final, he had played a huge part in the games before it. So, depending on the outcome of the match, Kang-in was eligible for either a gold or silver medal.

The Korea Republic players willed on Valencia and kept their fingers crossed for their teammate.

And, against the odds, Valencia won the match!

Two first half goals from Gameiro and Rodrigo had been enough to defeat Barcelona 1-2, with Lionel Messi's second half goal only a consolation for Barcelona.

Far away in Poland, Kang-in

celebrated with his teammates. He'd just won his first professional trophy! It was hard to grasp being so far away, but that didn't take away what Kang-in had already achieved. There would be a golden medal waiting for him on his return.

Kang-in's club triumph helped revitalise him for the rest of the tournament with Korea Republic. The team were able to put their opening day defeat behind them and emerge from the group, defeating South Africa 1-0 and then overcoming

Argentina 2-1. Korea Republic finished in second place and progressed to the knock-out rounds, where they would meet Japan.

Within Asian football, there is often a rivalry between Korea Republic and Japan. The two footballing powers of the region are always fighting for supremacy. So while this round of 16 tie was already important, it was even more important because of the opponent. Both sides were desperate to triumph over the other, to claim football bragging rights and knock their opponents out.

★ FOOTBALL RISING STARS ★

In a tough match, Korea Republic were able to defeat their rivals in a 1-0 triumph. A late goal from Oh Se-hun in the 84th minute was enough to send Kang-in and his country through to the quarter-finals.

Playing in top form, Korea Republic were willing to come up against any and every opponent that dared to get in their way.

They overcame Senegal in the quarter-finals, winning the close tie via a nerve-wracking penalty shoot-out, before defeating Ecuador 1-0 in the semi-final.

LEE KANG-IN

In an exciting final, Korea Republic would face off against Ukraine. Like Korea Republic, Ukraine had never reached the final of the U20 World Cup before. This meant a new country would be crowned as champions.

On the 15th of June 2019, Kang-in got his team off to the perfect start by scoring a penalty in the 5th minute. But a determined Ukraine team were able to fight back, eventually winning the match 3-1.

Kang-in and his teammates were disappointed. They had come so close and just missed out on the final day.

But the team had so much to be proud of. They had taken their country to its furthest point in the U20 World Cup – an achievement that would forever cement them as one of their country's best youth teams.

At the end of the final, the teams made their way to the podium to collect their medals.

But Kang-in knew that he would be going home with more than just a silver medal. He had played an instrumental part in his team's success, scoring two goals, providing four assists and impressing in

★ LEE KANG-IN ★

matches. Wowing those who watched him meant he had earned thousands of new fans. There was now a further awareness within the football community about a talented player for Korea Republic.

Many talented players had taken part in this competition. There was Erling Haaland, Darwin Nùñez, Amine Gouiri, Juliàn Álvarez and Rafael Leão – to name only a handful of rising stars at the tournament. Yet among this host of talent, it was

Kang-in who had shone the brightest.

Kang-in was given the Golden Ball, an award given to the best player at the tournament due to their hard work, talent and performances.

If audiences hadn't seen Kang-in before, they were certainly aware of him now. He was one of the best young talents in the world, earning the recognition he deserved on the biggest of international stages.

9
THE HURDLE

Kang-in enjoyed a small break after his U20 World Cup success. But after that, it was time to return to Valencia to reconnect with his club teammates and prepare for the 2019/2020 La Liga season.

He hoped to earn more minutes playing for the club, to continue his summer success and cement himself as a valuable player within the team. Kang-in pushed for this opportunity, training as well as he could, and he soon found himself on the team sheet.

Over the course of the season, he made seventeen appearances for the club in La Liga and scored two goals – one against Getafe and the other against Real Valladolid. Most of these appearances came in the form of substitutions, but it was an improvement on his debut season.

He was even able to make his Champions League debut in an away fixture against Chelsea at Stamford Bridge, becoming the youngest ever South Korean to make an appearance in the competition.

While Kang-in had made progress, it was a difficult La Liga campaign. The season was split in half following the outbreak of COVID-19, with many players stuck in lockdown as the world was brought to a halt. But after months of waiting, a sense of normality could resume and football matches could take place again. Valencia ended up finishing the league in ninth place.

The team took a break from football, before returning for the 2020/2021 season.

Kang-in was desperate to finally earn himself a spot as a regular starter. He was still one of the younger members of the team, but he had spent many years with the club now and felt that it was time to make the jump. In order for his career to move forward, he needed regular minutes in the first team.

★ LEE KANG-IN ★

There were a few reasons Kang-in never quite earned a regular first team spot, and all of them were out of his control. During a time of constant turbulence, multiple managers and changing styles, he was never seen as a first team player. He was a rising star with talent, a valuable player, but the managers couldn't fit him into their systems on a regular basis.

With his contract coming to an end after the 2020/2021 season, Kang-in had a decision to make. Should he renew his contract with Valencia, or continue his career somewhere else?

It was a very difficult decision, especially because Kang-in did not want to leave. The club was like a second home to him. It was somewhere he had spent years learning, developing and growing.

But everything can't always go to plan. Kang-in had played his very best for Valencia but never quite earned that starting spot. The way forward was to play in every match and push himself to new limits, so he came to the conclusion that he needed to play

LEE KANG-IN

for another team in order to further his career.

Valencia offered numerous renewals, but Kang-in's mind could not be changed. It was time to leave his second home. He had joined the club as a boy moving across the world, and now he was leaving as a young professional player.

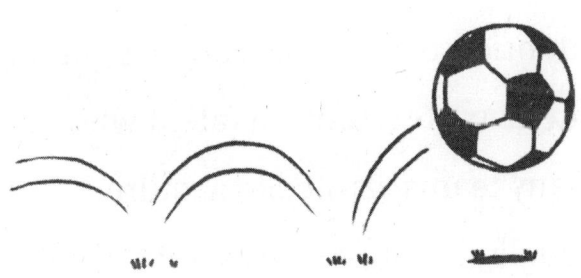

10
RCD MALLORCA

There were plenty of teams interested in signing Kang-in.

He hadn't quite yet caught the attention of some of football's giants, but he was certainly a talent who many teams wanted to acquire. Equally, because he was not tied down

LEE KANG-IN

by a contract, any new team wouldn't need to part with a transfer fee.

Instead, they'd be able to sign a free agent, offering tempting wages and a signing bonus to try and beat any competition.

Yet finances were not the only thing that would help make up Kang-in's mind. He had chosen to leave Valencia for a reason: to get his name on the team sheet on a regular basis. Any new team needed to be the right fit for Kang-in. They needed to have a space in their first team and believe that the developing young player was their missing puzzle piece.

After considering multiple offers and discussing them with his agent, family and friends, Kang-in came to his decision.

He would be getting on a plane, flying away and starting his next chapter in a new location. This time, however, Kang-in would not need to learn a new language.

He had chosen to sign for RCD Mallorca, a team that had just earned promotion from the Segunda División to compete in La Liga.

★ **LEE KANG-IN** ★

The team were not based in mainland Spain, but rather on an island called Mallorca. It was a destination tourists often visited to enjoy the sandy beaches, sheltered coves and blue seas. This beautiful island was Kang-in's new home, and there would be plenty of opportunities to explore it.

But first, Kang-in wanted to get back onto a football pitch and kick-start his career, making the most of his fresh start at a new football club.

Despite still being young, Kang-in was brought in as one of the team's key players – an attacking force who could help them avoid relegation from the top division.

The club held up their side of the bargain, and Kang-in was an important player for the team throughout the 2021/2022 season. While he didn't break scoring or assist tally records, he made a strong impact and helped his team when they needed him most. He was a bundle of energy!

In a tough season, Kang-in repaid the club's faith by helping them

★ **LEE KANG-IN** ★

narrowly avoid relegation. The side just finished above the drop by a single point.

Each and every point was hard-earned, and Kang-in finally felt like a full-time professional football player. He was a member of the squad who could be trusted to play in most matches, rather than having to watch from the sidelines and cross his fingers for a short substitute appearance.

Kang-in's reputation was growing by the day, and he had timed it perfectly. The 2022 World Cup was just around the corner. This time, the famous tournament was taking place in Qatar.

Had Kang-in done enough to book his ticket?

11
WORLD CUP 2022

World Cup competitions usually take place over the summer, between the break for the majority of professional football leagues. However, the 2022 World Cup was breaking that mould.

It was to be hosted in Qatar, where summer temperatures can exceed forty-three degrees, so it was agreed that a summer tournament would not be possible. Instead, the tournament would take place over winter. This meant that the players didn't have to put their health at risk by playing sport at extreme temperatures. Plus, it also meant that millions of travelling supporters would be able to enjoy the fiesta of football more comfortably.

While this solved one problem, it caused another. Many football leagues would have to pause for the

★ LEE KANG-IN ★

competition, and the 2021/2022 La Liga season was no exception.

Kang-in continued to pick up minutes for RCD Mallorca in the league, helping the team improve upon the previous season and look higher up the table. As well as continuing his form, he added more goals and assists to his game.

His hard work in La Liga had impressed the national team coaches, and there were rumours that he would make it into Korea Republic's first team for the World Cup.

When the time came, Kang-in was worried that he hadn't done enough to earn his place in the squad after all … But he had!

Kang-in was selected as part of Korea Republic's team! He had represented his country in youth tournaments before, but he had yet to play for the Korea Republic in a major international competition. To play for his country in the most watched and admired tournament in the world was better than he could've ever imagined.

★ LEE KANG-IN ★

Kang-in joined up with all of his teammates in Qatar. In order to prepare for the competition, the squad were staying in a hotel with impressive training facilities.

By this point, World Cup fever was in full effect, with millions – if not billions – of fans across the world excited for the tournament to begin. The Korea Republic team, filled with talented stars, were also itching to get started.

Korea Republic had been drawn into Group H with Uruguay, Ghana and Portugal. It was a tough

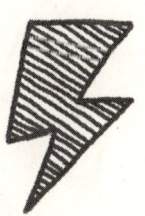

group and, like Korea Republic, every team believed they had what it took to emerge victorious.

To progress to the knock-out rounds, Korea Republic would have to earn enough points to come first or second in the group table. It was certainly not going to be easy, but this Korea Republic team believed in themselves. Kang-in was incredibly proud to be in Qatar, so he was going to do everything he could to push his side as far as they could go.

★ LEE KANG-IN ★

After lots of waiting, Korea Republic's first match of the tournament arrived. The fixture was against Uruguay at the Education City Stadium in Al Rayann. 41,663 fans made their way to the stadium. Some fans had painted their faces or were wearing their country's colours with pride, while others held banners with supportive messages. The atmosphere was filled with excitement and nervous energy. Kang-in, although in the squad, was not named in the starting eleven.

He had to settle for a place on the bench, watching the match unfold before him in the hope that he would eventually get an opportunity to make his World Cup debut.

Neither side were able to make a breakthrough, with defence defying attack for both sides. Kang-in was eventually brought into the match late on. But with his limited minutes, he was unable to break the deadlock.

At the end of the game, both sides had earned one point. It wasn't the three they wanted, but it was still a solid foundation to build upon. For now, both sides' dreams of knock-out football were kept alive.

However, Korea Republic's second match did not go to plan. In a hotly contested tie, Ghana emerged as the victors in a 3-2 win. Kang-in started on the bench once again, but he was introduced early in the second half. Although he provided an assist for a goal, that was not enough to win the dramatic fixture.

Korea Republic's hopes were not completely dashed. They still had a chance to progress to the knock-out rounds. They just needed to perform well in their final group match against Portugal, and hope that the fixture between Uruguay and Ghana also went in their favour.

Portugal were already qualified, so they were not in desperate need of points, whereas the Korea Republic had to win to stand any chance of progression.

But the Portuguese team, led by Cristiano Ronaldo, would not just be rolling over. Any match in the World

★ LEE KANG-IN ★

Cup is an exciting opportunity for a player, and winning everything you can is crucial.

Who out of Ghana, Uruguay or Korea Republic would get the job done and claim second place?

This time, Kang-in was chosen to be in the starting eleven. The coach understood the impact Kang-in could make and had decided to rely on him for this crucial tie. Unfortunately, things got off to a terrible start. Portugal found the net in the 5th minute thanks to

Ricardo Horta, but Kang-in and his teammates were not going to give up. There were still so many minutes yet to play!

The team created an opportunity in the 27th minute. Kim Young-gwon swept home an equaliser after the ball fell to him following a corner.

As things stood, Korea Republic would still be eliminated from the competition. Only a win and good fortune in the other fixture would be enough.

Kang-in and his teammates tried to score the winner, but no matter how

hard they tried they struggled to find it. Growing tired, Kang-in was substituted late in the game to make way for fresh legs. The team pushed and pushed, trying to create one last opportunity.

In the 91st minute, they had a chance. Son latched onto a loose ball and drove at the Portuguese defence. Despite being surrounded by players, he was going to do everything he could to reach that goal.

On the bench, Kang-in moved

forward – as did the rest of the coaching team willing their team on.

Son was joined by a late run from Hwang Hee-chan. Son played the ball to Hwang Hee-chan in the penalty area, who then slotted the ball into the net. They were in the lead! The stadium erupted with cheers from the Korea Republic fans. The team held onto the lead and won the fixture.

But progression was still not guaranteed. It depended on the outcome of the Ghana vs Uruguay

★ **LEE KANG-IN** ★

game. Uruguay were winning 2-0, and as it stood that was enough for Korea Republic. But one more goal for Uruguay would change that.

The Korea Republic players gathered around a stream of the match on a mobile phone to watch. And after a nervy few minutes, the game was over. Uruguay had not scored a third goal, so Korea Republic would be going through to the knock-outs! The players on the pitch celebrated as if they had won the entire competition. It had looked unlikely at the start of the day, but this team had achieved it. Their tournament continued.

However, Kang-in and his teammates would only play one more match. In a tricky round of 16 tie, Korea Republic were eliminated by Brazil, who were one of the tournament favourites. The team lost 4-1.

Kang-in's World Cup journey had come to an end. While he was disappointed, he was also incredibly proud of the role he had played. He had showed millions

★ LEE KANG-IN ★

of onlookers exactly what he could do, helping his team enjoy magical moments he'd cherish forever.

Still being so young, it was certain that Kang-in would receive more chances in his career. One day, he would get another shot to lead Korea Republic to glory in a major international tournament.

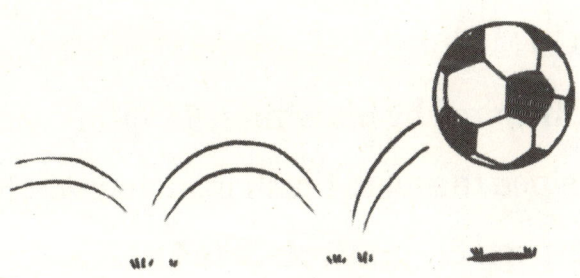

PARIS SAINT-GERMAIN

Kang-in returned from the winter tournament and regrouped with RCD Mallorca.

Inspired by his winter, Kang-in helped the team finish in an incredibly respectable ninth place in La Liga.

LEE KANG-IN

The team were far from relegation and only a few places away from the European competition spots.

Kang-in was loving his time at his new club. He felt as if he was heading in the right direction, and those from afar believed that he was too. The star from South Korea attracted a lot of transfer interest over the summer of 2023. Kang-in had not planned on leaving RCD Mallorca, but an offer came in that made him seriously consider it.

Paris Saint-Germain (PSG), one of the biggest football clubs in France, saw something in Kang-in. The Parisian club believed that he would be a good fit for their team and offered €22 million. Would RCD Mallorca accept?

The money was a lot for the club, and although they did not want to part with Kang-in, RCD Mallorca were happy with the terms. Kang-in was ecstatic about the prospect of playing for such a great team, so it didn't take too much persuading to encourage him to make the move.

Kang-in's time at RCD Mallorca had come to an end. It had been the

★ LEE KANG-IN ★

perfect place for him to regain his confidence and pick up valuable minutes. Leaving the comfort of Valencia had been a bold move, but it had more than paid off. RCD Mallorca would always be a special club for Kang-in, but it was time for another adventure.

Kang-in collected his things and moved to France, joining up with his teammates in the nation's capital. But he wasn't given long to settle in.

Almost before he could unpack his bags, it was time to move again.

★ **FOOTBALL RISING STARS** ★

Kang-in headed overseas with his club on a pre-season tour. PSG were going to Japan to prepare for the upcoming season, playing matches against talented clubs from across the world. After having a short break from their seasons and holidays with family, the trip would give the players time to regain fitness and help the club gain more fans.

In recent years, PSG had been a club filled with superstars, with the likes of Kylian Mbappé, Lionel Messi and Neymar wearing the shirt – an impressive trio of attackers who were seen by many as some of the best football players in the world. PSG were a team that hosted megastars who dreamt of winning it all, and yet this team of stars appeared to be in transition.

Messi had recently departed for Inter Miami, Mbappé was in a contract dispute and it had been rumoured that Neymar was looking to move. This left PSG the tough task of replacing some of the best.

Kang-in knew that he had a long way to go to reach the heights of those stars, but this was a challenge that he was not going to shy away from. He was going to prove that he deserved to play with the best and could *be* the best – to wear the blue, red and white of PSG.

In Japan, the team played in friendlies against Al-Nassr, Cerezo Osaka and Inter Milan. However, none of those matches were major hits. Thousands attended, but not quite as many as hoped.

Still, the team's pre-season tour wasn't entirely over. A late addition had been put on the team's schedule. PSG would be making their way over

★ LEE KANG-IN ★

to South Korea to play in a friendly against Jeonbuk Hyundai Motors!

Kang-in was going to get to play for his new team in his home country, and he couldn't wait. And it appeared that the fans couldn't wait either.

PSG's match in South Korea was a huge success. The stands were filled with new fans wearing PSG shirts, many of which had Kang-in's name on the back of them. Before the game started, there had been a line believed to be half a kilometre long in order to buy PSG merchandise!

Kang-in started on the bench, but that didn't stop fans chanting his name. When he was finally brought into the match in the 69th minute, the stadium erupted into cheers and applause. He helped his team to an incredible 0-3 victory.

PSG might well be losing some of their stars, but it appeared that a new one was starting to shine. There were big boots to fill, but Kang-in was going to give it his best shot and make his mark as a rising star for PSG.

13
ASIAN GAMES

Before Kang-in could get stuck into competitive life at PSG, there was something else he needed to do.

With the club's permission, Kang-in was allowed to join up with Korea Republic's U23s side for the Asian Games – known as Hangzhou 2022. Not dissimilar from the Olympics, the competition takes place every four years and is where the best athletes from Asia compete in their chosen sports. The tournament for this cycle was taking place in China in the summer of 2023, following a one-year postponement due to COVID-19.

Korea Republic had been drawn into Group E. Kang-in and his teammates would need to gain enough points to progress in matches against Bahrain, Thailand and Kuwait. As heavy favourites, Korea Republic were expected to make it out of the group.

⋆★ LEE KANG-IN ★⋆

Kang-in and his teammates did not disappoint, putting on strong performances to blow away the opposition. They won all three matches, scored sixteen goals and conceded none. This outstanding performance put Korea Republic in strong contention for the title.

No side wanted to be drawn against them in the knock-out rounds, and this fear was realised when Kang-in and his teammates bulldozed through every team they faced. They eliminated

Kyrgyzstan, China and Uzbekistan to make it all the way to the final of the competition, setting up an exciting tie against Japan.

It was going to be a tough battle for the two ferocious sides. For whoever could better the other, a glorious prize awaited them: the chance to be crowned as Asian Games champions and end the day with a golden medal.

A part of Korea Republic's eleven, Kang-in was going to do everything he could to triumph for his country.

Despite the team's efforts, Japan were able to sneak ahead. An early

★ LEE KANG-IN ★

goal from Kotaro Uchino gave Japan the advantage. But there was still a lot of football to play, and this Korea Republic team never gave up the fight.

In the 27th minute, the team found an equaliser through Jeong Woo-yeong. The midfielder found the back of the net with a confident header to bring his country back into the game.

Things then got even better in the 56th minute, when Cho Young-wook was able to put Korea Republic ahead. He coolly slotted the ball into the goal, sending the visiting fans into cheers and applause.

Kang-in's team were able to hold onto the lead and celebrate an incredible achievement. Korea Republic had now won the men's football tournament in the Asian Games three times in a row!

On a personal note, the victory was crucial for the Korea Republic players' careers. Now that they had brought sporting honour to their country, they would not have to take time out of the game to serve in the military.

All men in South Korea between the ages of eighteen and thirty-five must serve at least eighteen months

★ LEE KANG-IN ★

in the military service. However, athletes who triumph in certain competitions such as the Asian Games or Olympics do not have to join.

This was important for Kang-in, as a football player's career is only so long. Due to his success, he no longer had to worry about leaving the game during his peak years. Instead, all he had to worry about was where he was going to place his new golden medal in his Parisian home.

14
HOPE AND BELIEF

Kang-in has now returned to Paris and is making an impact for PSG.

As for any player, there was a period of settling and change, but it appears that he is starting to feel comfortable in his new surroundings.

On the 3rd of January 2024, Kang-in

scored the opening goal in the delayed 2023 Trophée des Champions game against Toulouse. PSG went on to win 2-0, and Kang-in was named as the Man of the Match!

From then on, things only got better. By the end of the 2023/2024 season, PSG had won Ligue 1 and the Coupe de France. They were knocked out of the Champions League by German giants Borussia Dortmund in the semi-final, but the team are determined to try again in the upcoming season.

Kang-in has been welcomed into Paris with open arms by the fans. The club has been the home of multiple superstars in recent years, and now he's one of them.

Thousands of fans across the world wear their Kang-in shirts with pride, showing their support for the young star representing South Korea on the world stage. As an extraordinary talent, he has earned this supportive fanbase.

Messi, Neymar and Mbappé may have left PSG, but the club have unearthed a new generation of talent. At the forefront is Kang-in, an exciting player with lots of potential. It may be too soon to compare him to the greats, but he is already providing unforgettable moments that only football can create. No matter his future, Kang-in will excite and amaze supporters worldwide.

Players have taken many different paths into the professional game, but none have forged their way in quite the same way as Kang-in. He has come so far since his early days on *Fly Shoot Dori*. He has flown across the globe and lived in Spain, represented Korea Republic in international tournaments and finally signed for one of the world's biggest football teams. He is an inspiration for all young children across the world.

But most importantly, he is a shining example that football is a global sport. One where anyone, no matter where they're born, can make it to the very top.

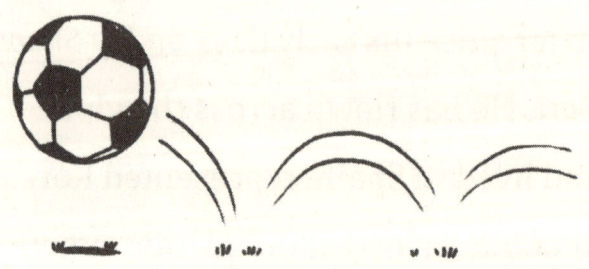